JAZZ GUITAR CHORD MELODY SOLOS

Christmas Carols

Arrangements by Masa Takahashi

ISBN 978-1-4234-9478-2

HAL•LEONARD®
CORPORATION

7777 W. BLUEMOUND RD. P.O. BOX 13819 MILWAUKEE, WI 53213

Christmas Carols

4	Angels from the Realms of Glory
6	Angels We Have Heard on High
8	Auld Lang Syne
5	Away in a Manger
10	Deck the Hall
12	The First Noel
14	God Rest Ye Merry, Gentlemen
16	Good Christian Men, Rejoice
13	Good King Wenceslas
18	Hark! The Herald Angels Sing
20	Here We Come A-Wassailing
21	It Came Upon the Midnight Clear
22	Jingle Bells
24	Joy to the World
25	O Christmas Tree
26	O Come, All Ye Faithful (Adeste Fideles)
27	O Come, O Come Immanuel
28	O Holy Night
30	O Little Town of Bethlehem
31	Silent Night
34	Toyland
32	The Twelve Days of Christmas
35	Up on the Housetop
36	We Three Kings of Orient Are
37	We Wish You a Merry Christmas
38	What Child Is This?

Angels from the Realms of Glory

Words by James Montgomery
Music by Henry T. Smart

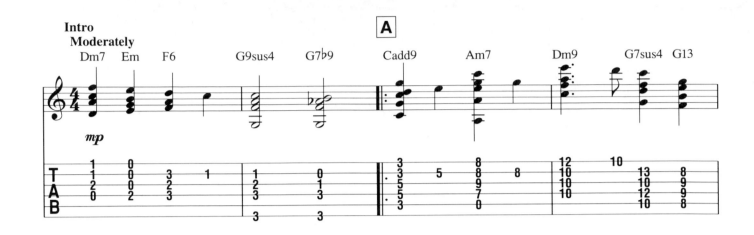

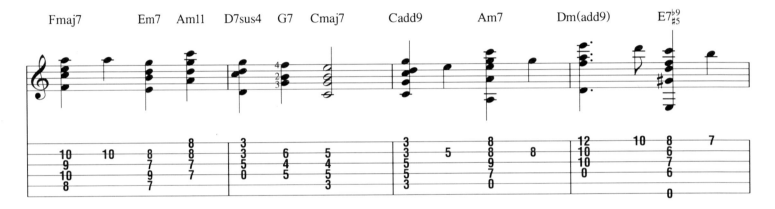

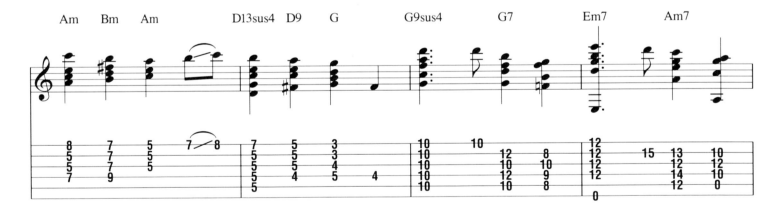

Away in a Manger

Words by John T. McFarland (v.3)
Music by James R. Murray

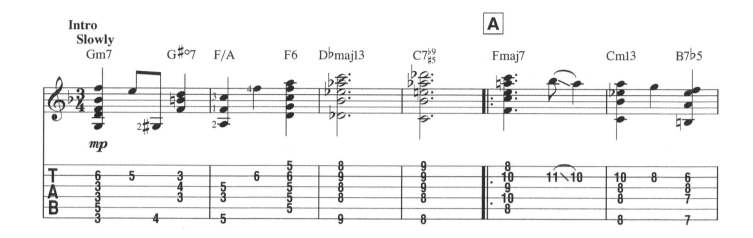

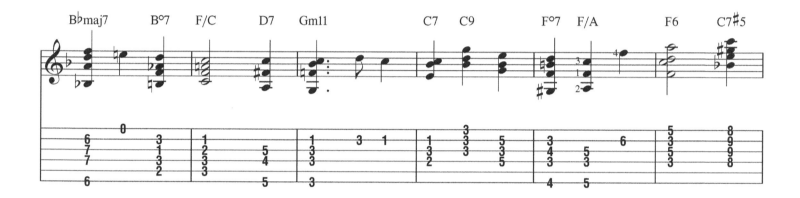

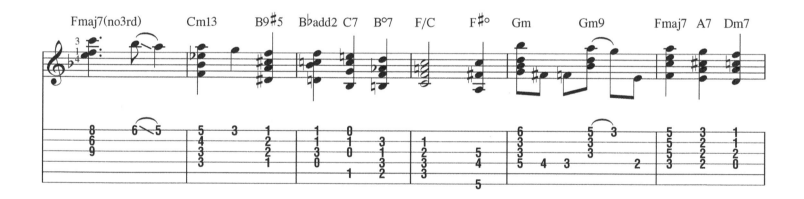

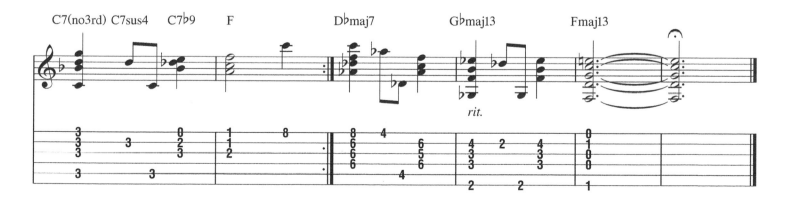

Angels We Have Heard on High

Traditional French Carol
Translated by James Chadwick

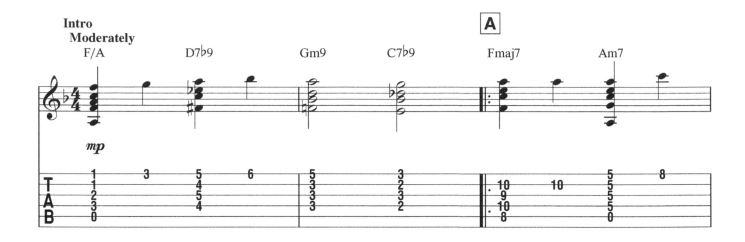

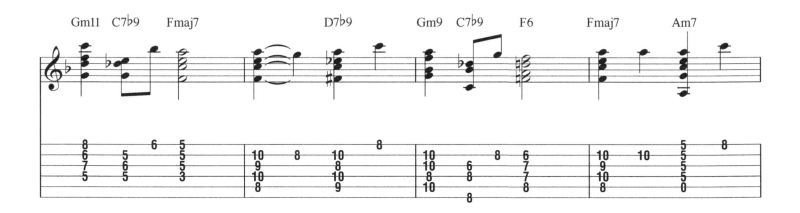

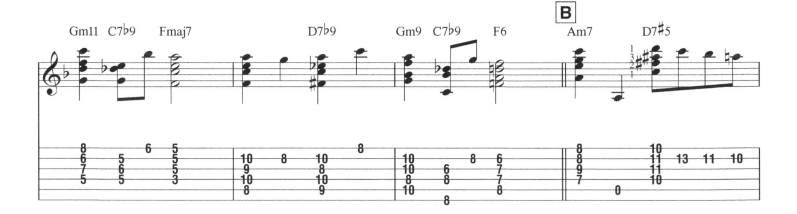

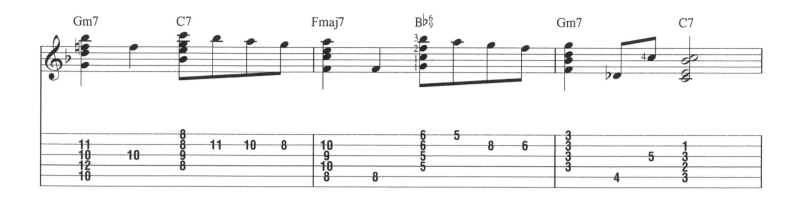

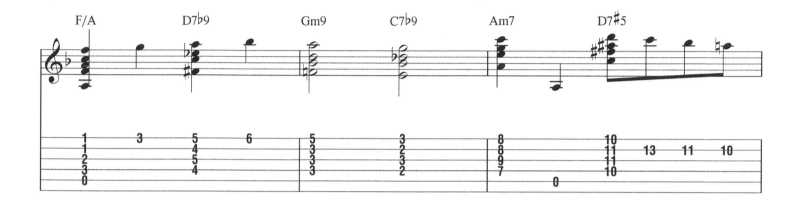

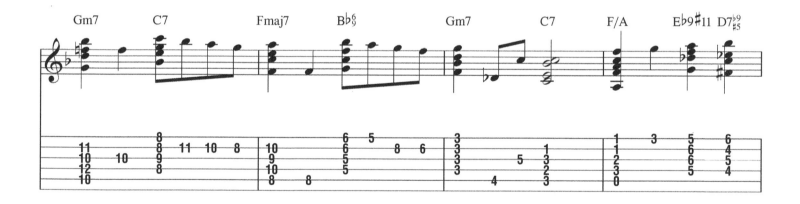

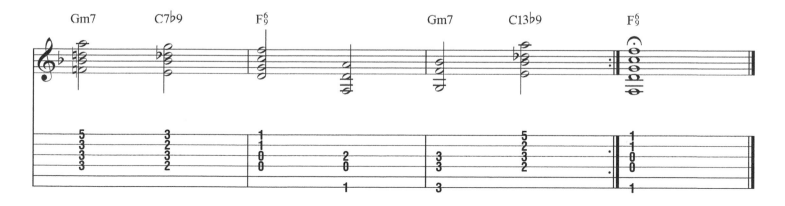

Auld Lang Syne

Words by Robert Burns
Traditional Scottish Melody

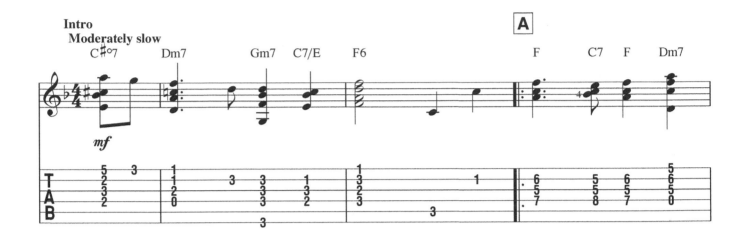

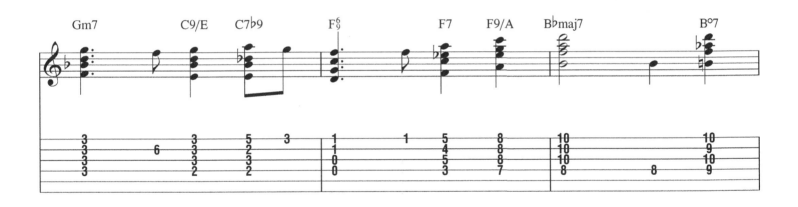

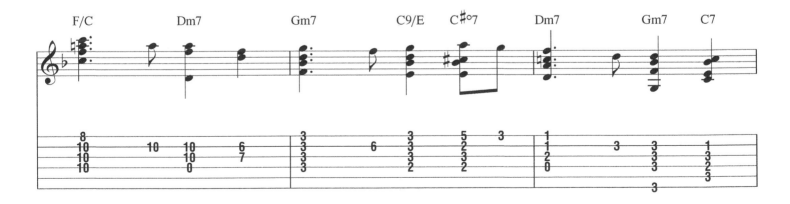

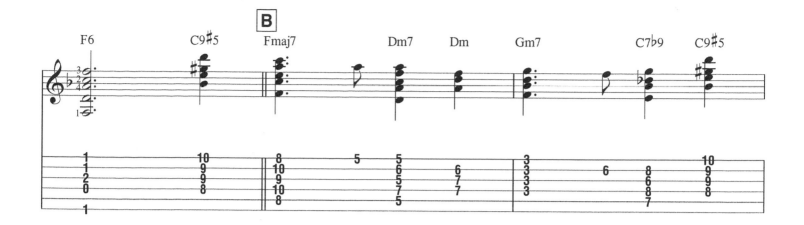

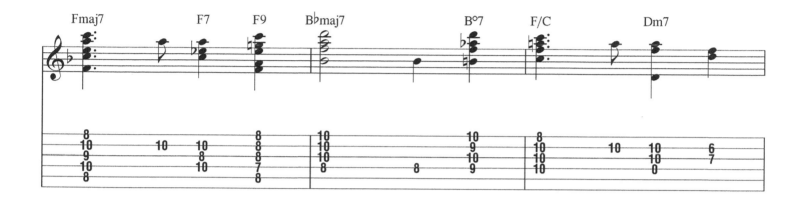

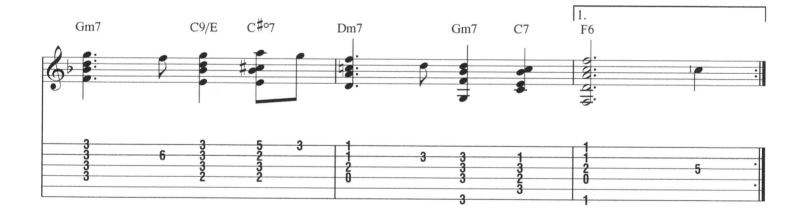

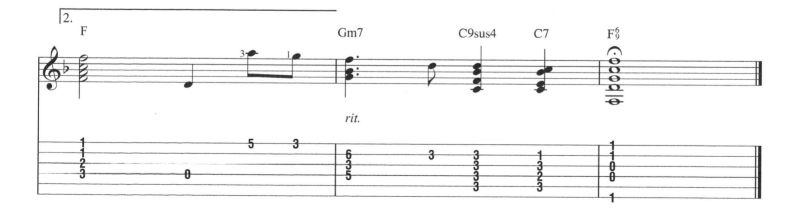

Deck the Hall

Traditional Welsh Carol

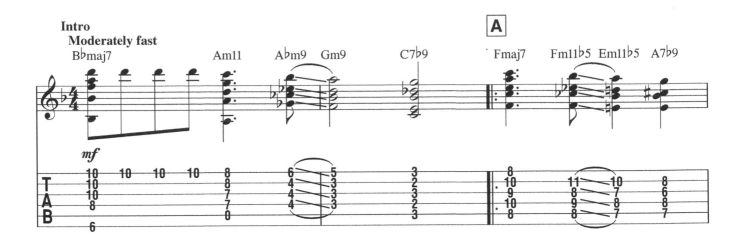

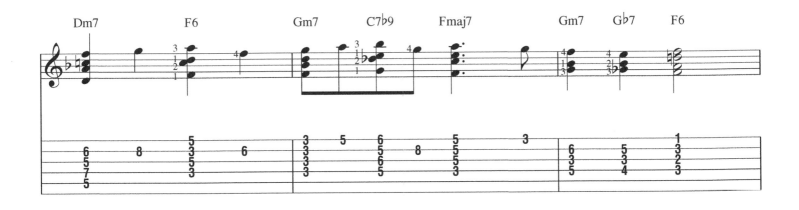

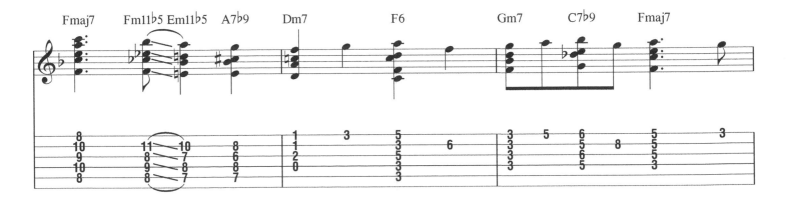

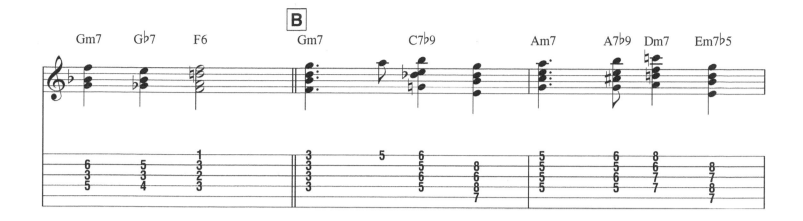

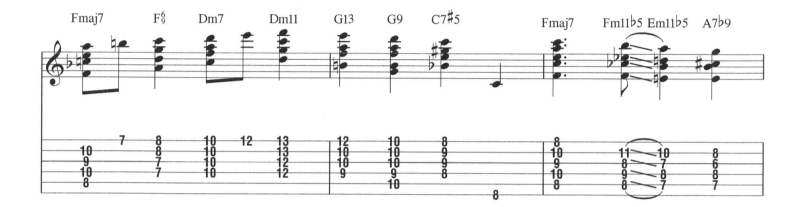

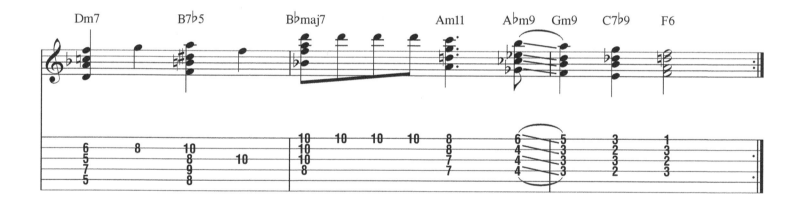

Outro

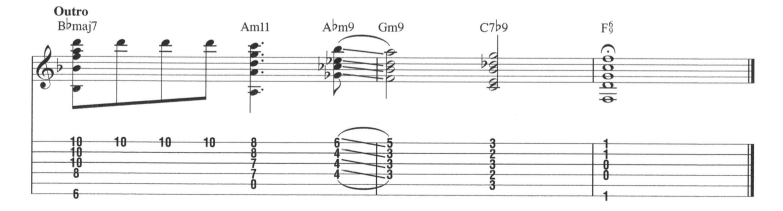

The First Noel

17th Century English Carol
Music from W. Sandys' Christmas Carols

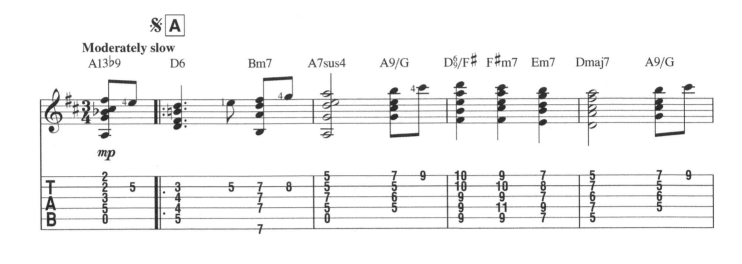

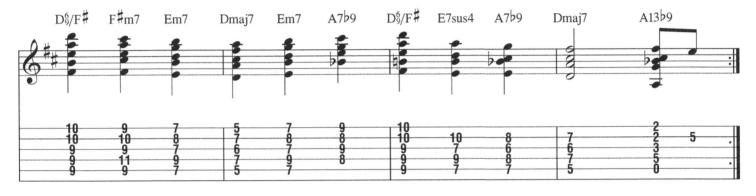

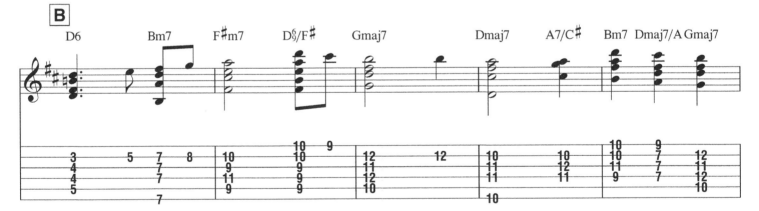

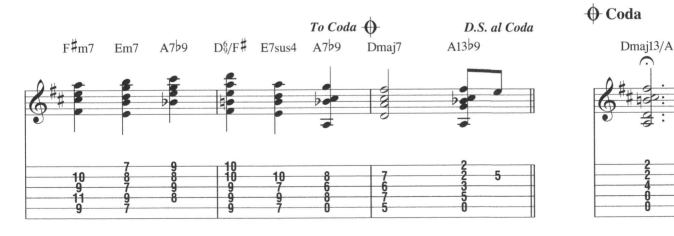

Good King Wenceslas

Words by John M. Neale
Music from Piae Cantiones

God Rest Ye Merry, Gentlemen

19th Century English Carol

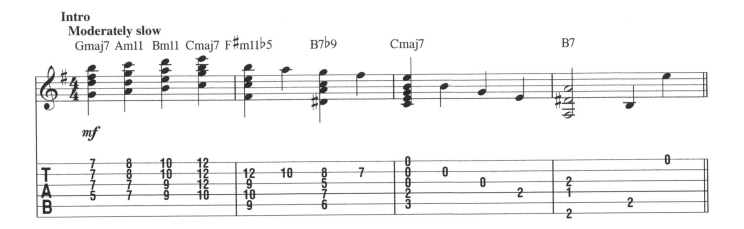

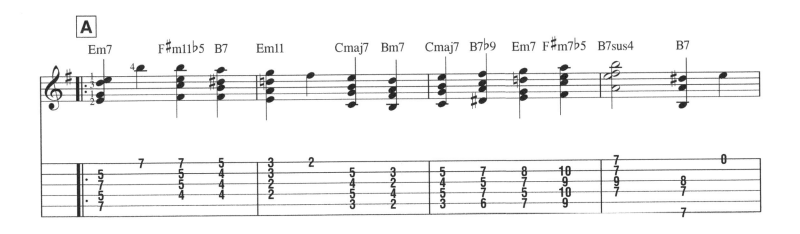

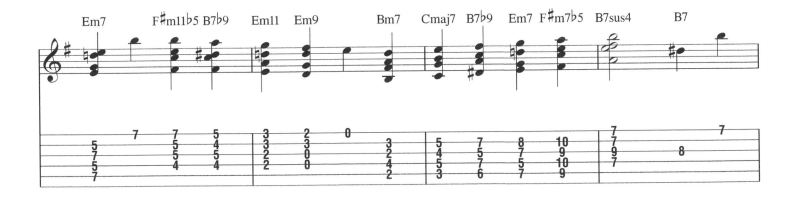

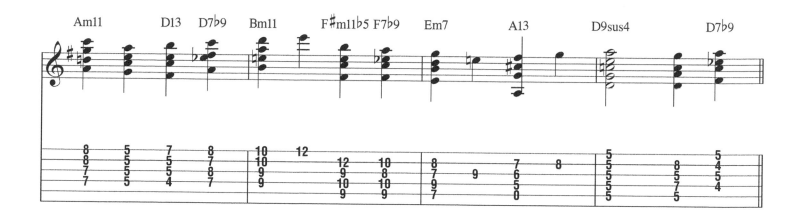

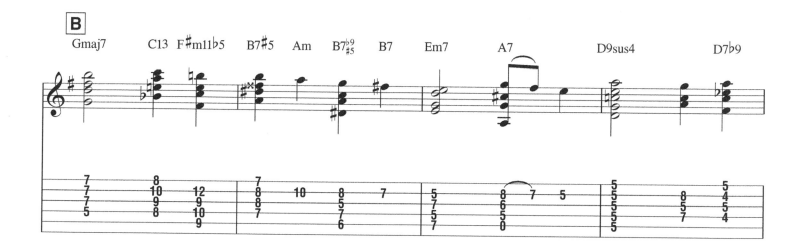

Good Christian Men, Rejoice

14th Century Latin Text
Translated by John Mason Neale
14th Century German Melody

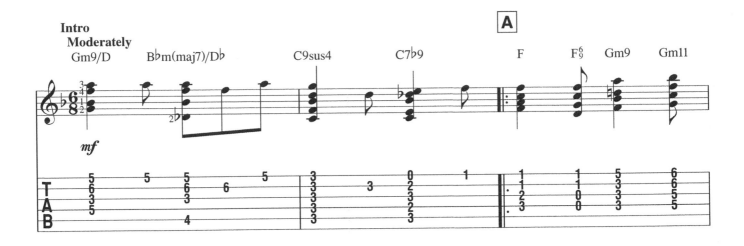

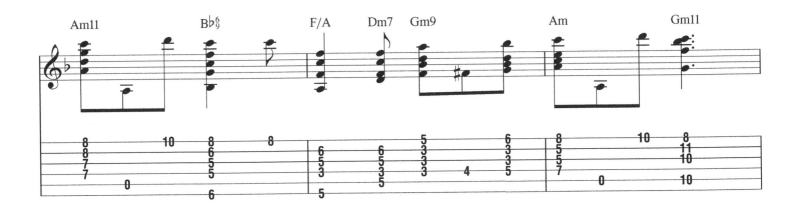

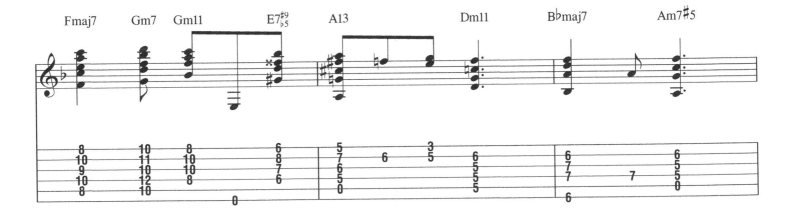

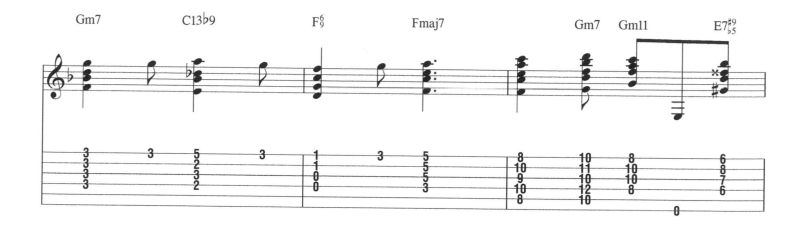

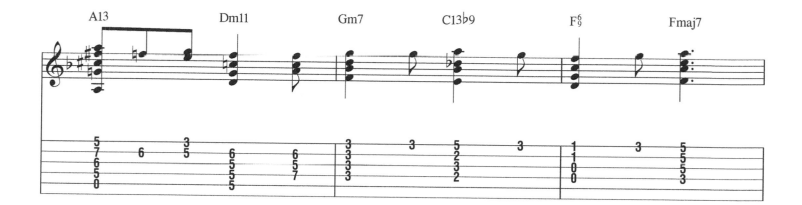

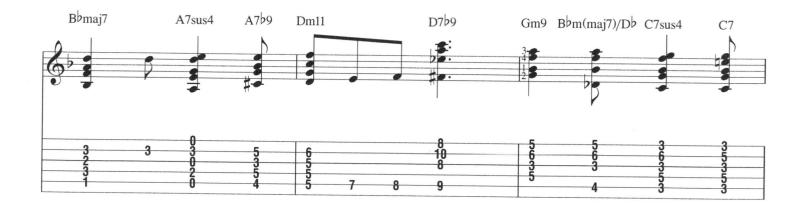

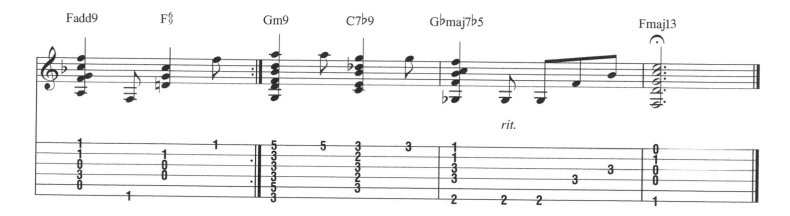

Hark! The Herald Angels Sing

Words by Charles Wesley
Altered by George Whitefield
Music by Felix Mendelssohn-Bartholdy
Arranged by William H. Cummings

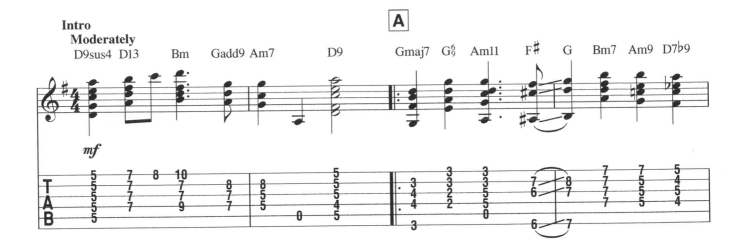

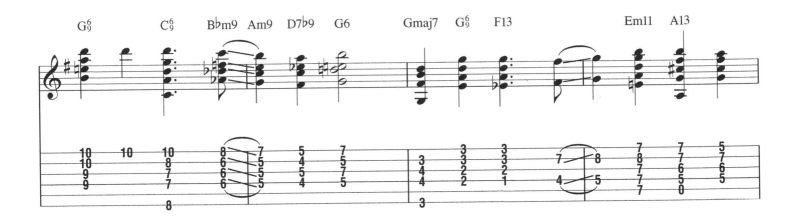

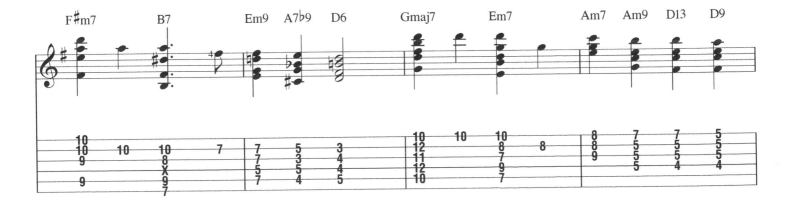

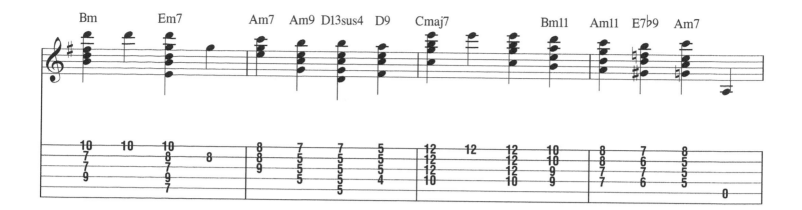

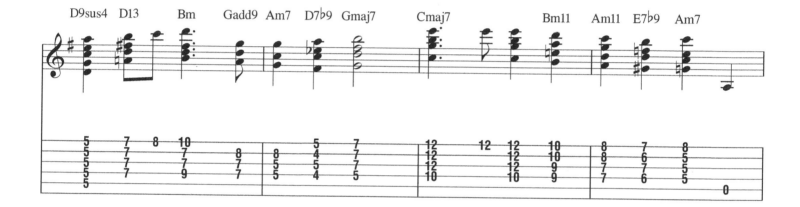

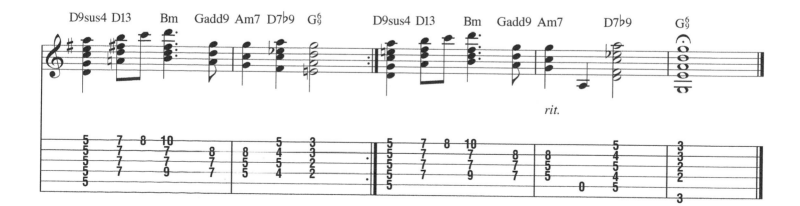

Here We Come A-Wassailing

Traditional

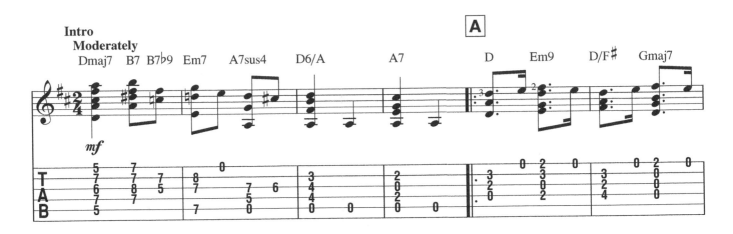

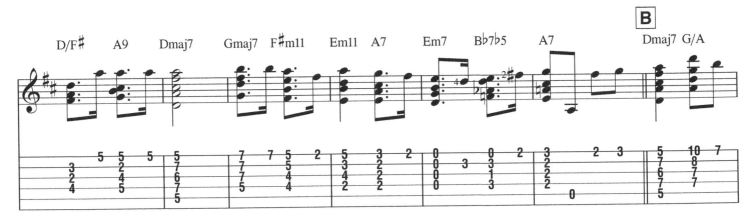

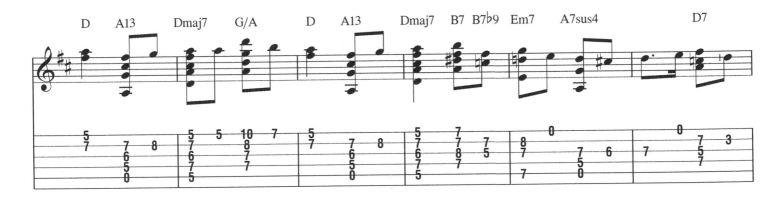

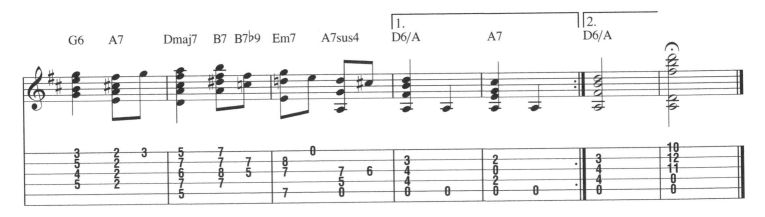

It Came Upon the Midnight Clear

Words by Edmund Hamilton Sears
Music by Richard Storrs Willis

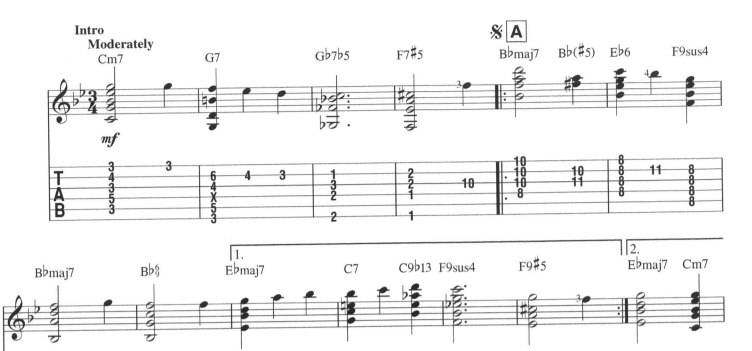

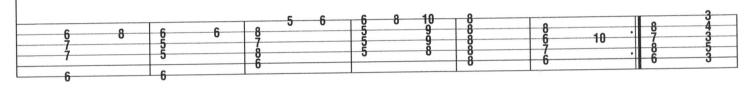

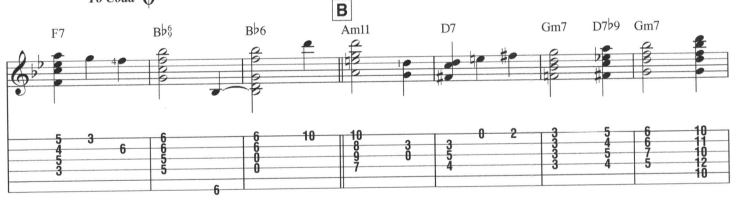

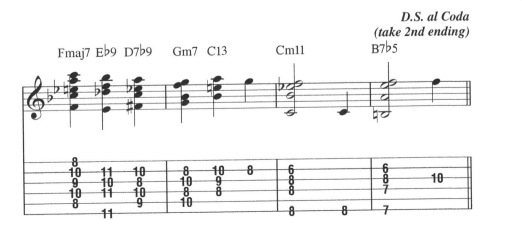

Jingle Bells

Words and Music by J. Pierpont

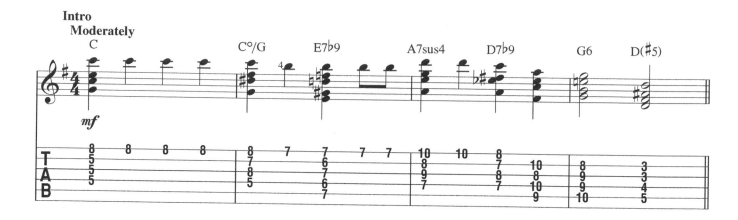

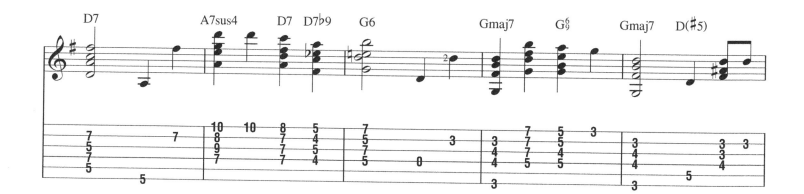

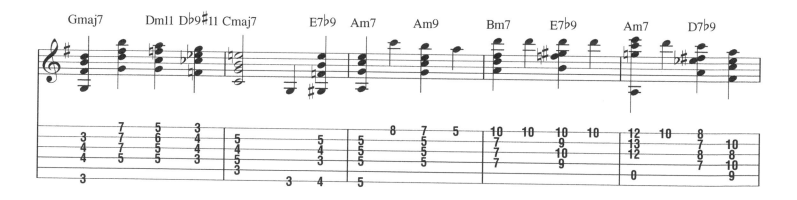

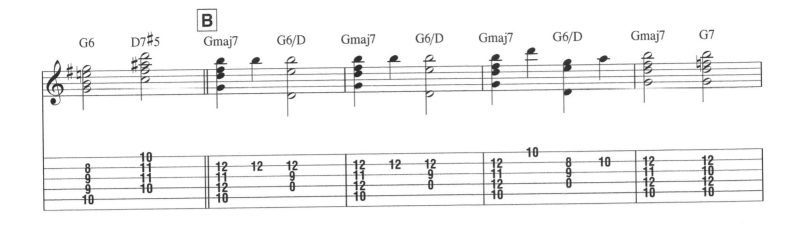

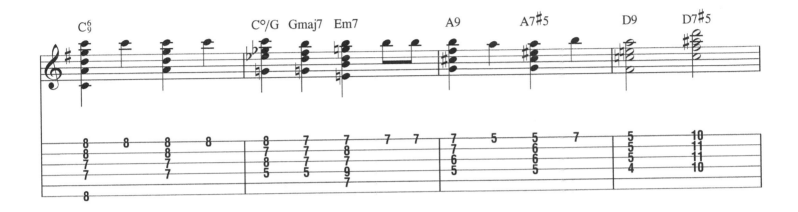

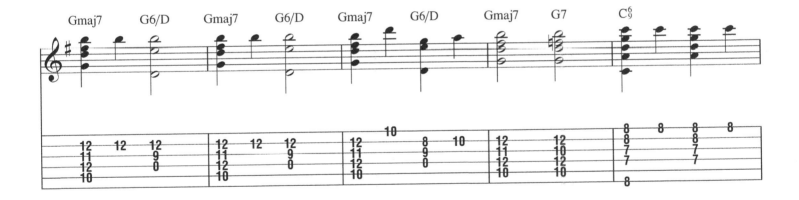

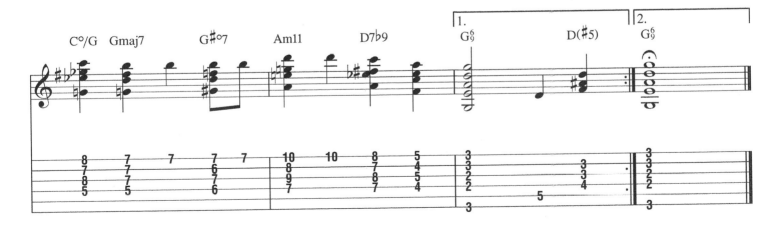

Joy to the World

Words by Isaac Watts
Music by George Frideric Handel
Adapted by Lowell Mason

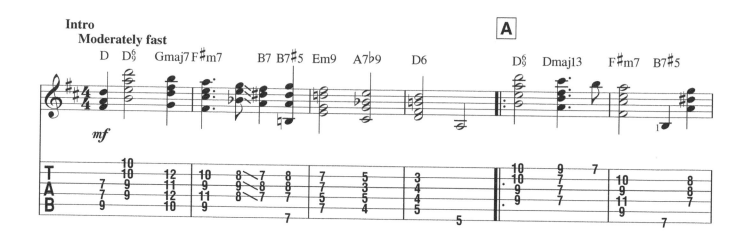

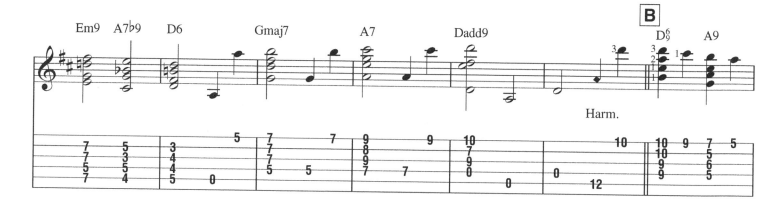

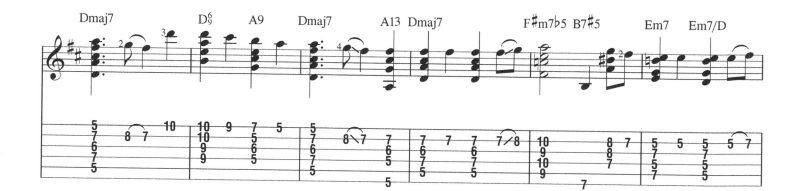

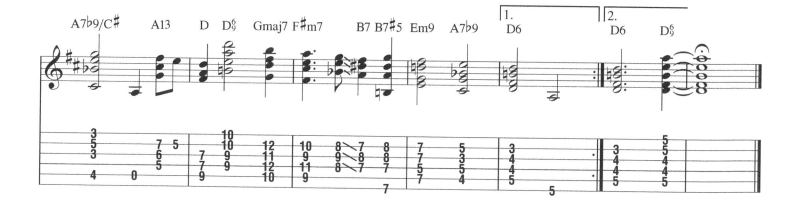

O Christmas Tree

Traditional German Carol

O Come, All Ye Faithful

(Adeste Fideles)

Music by John Francis Wade
Latin Words translated by Frederick Oakeley

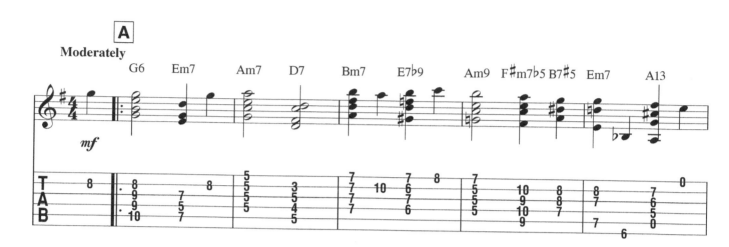

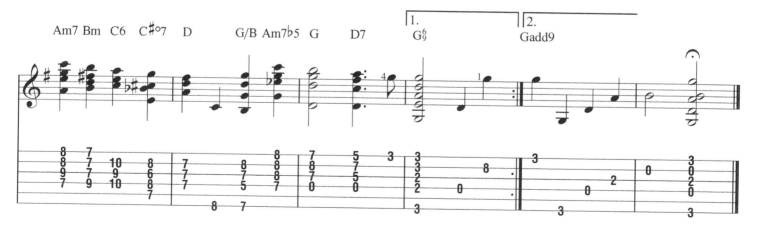

O Come, O Come Immanuel

Plainsong, 13th Century
Words translated by John M. Neale and Henry S. Coffin

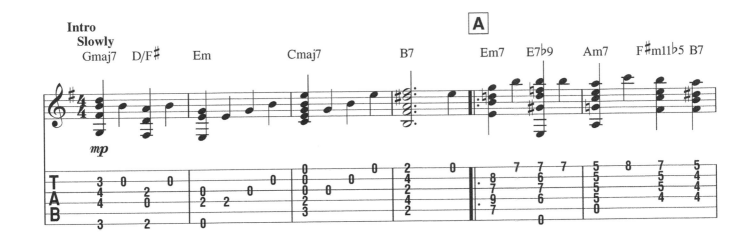

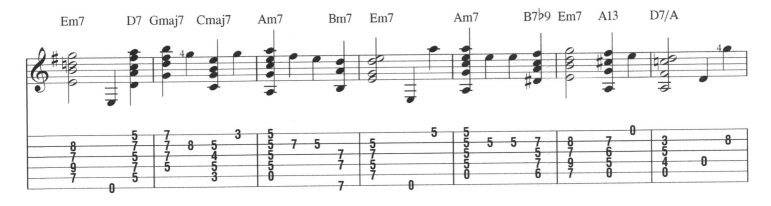

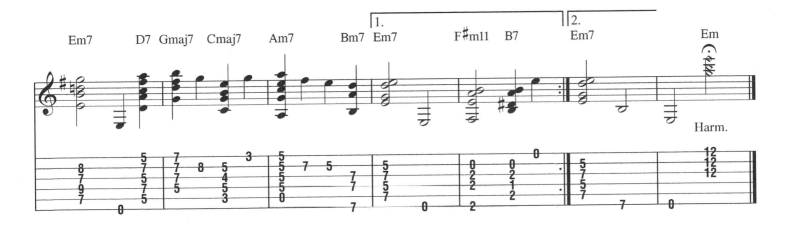

O Holy Night

French Words by Placide Cappeau
English Words by John S. Dwight
Music by Adolphe Adam

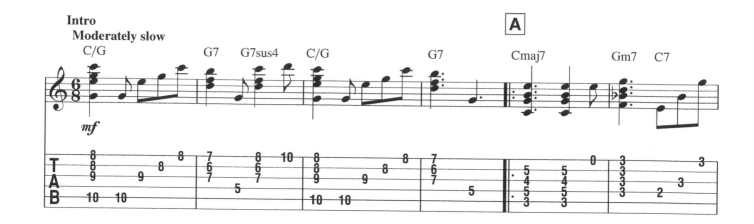

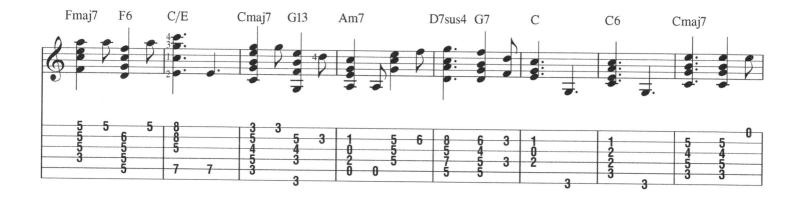

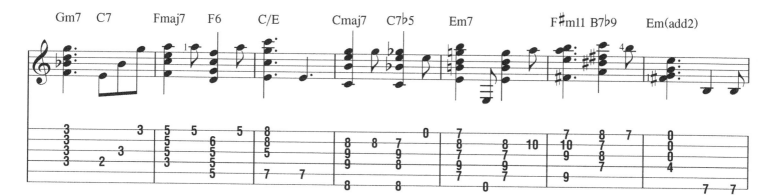

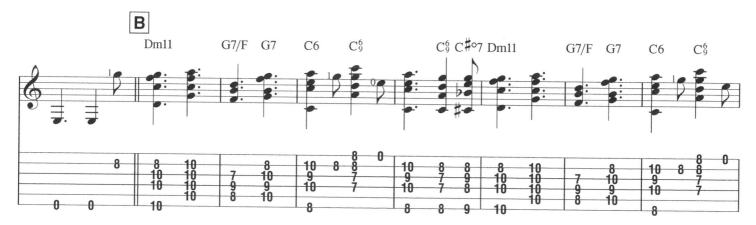

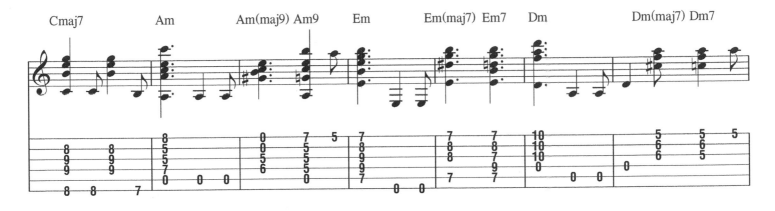

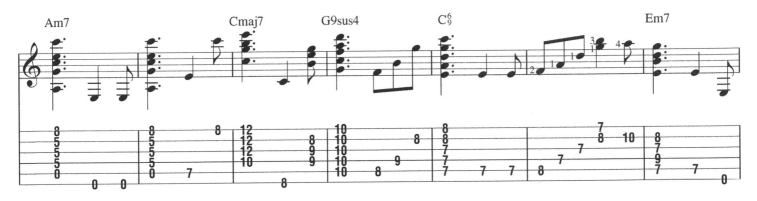

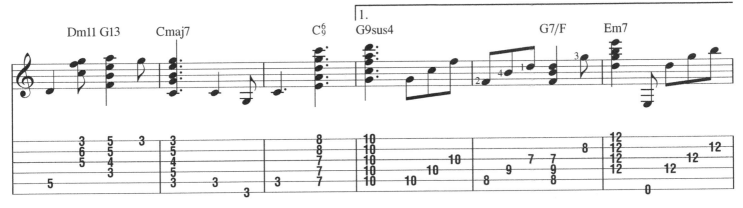

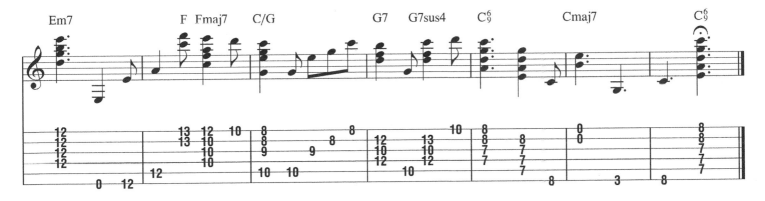

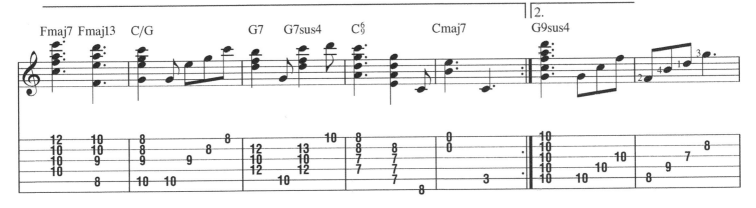

O Little Town of Bethlehem

Words by Phillips Brooks
Music by Lewis H. Redner

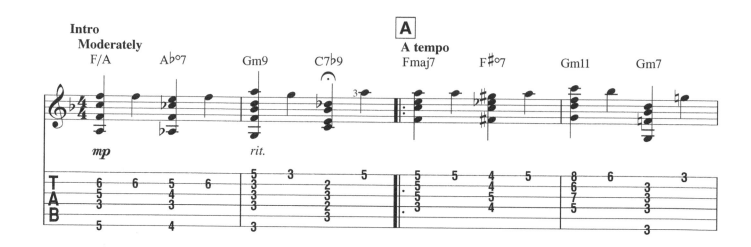

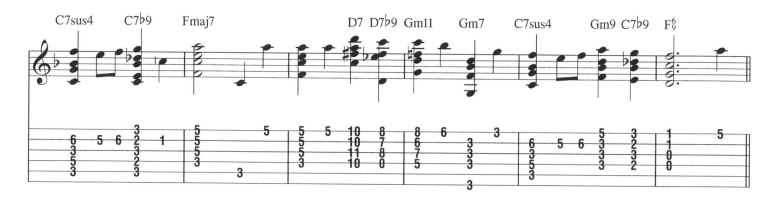

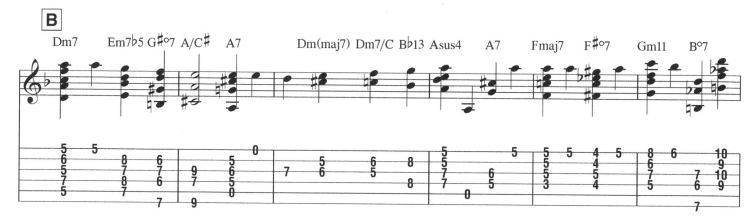

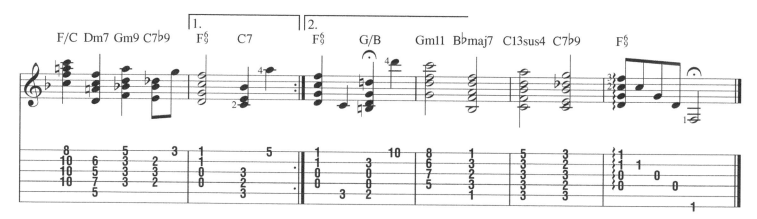

Silent Night

Words by Joseph Mohr
Translated by John F. Young
Music by Franz X. Gruber

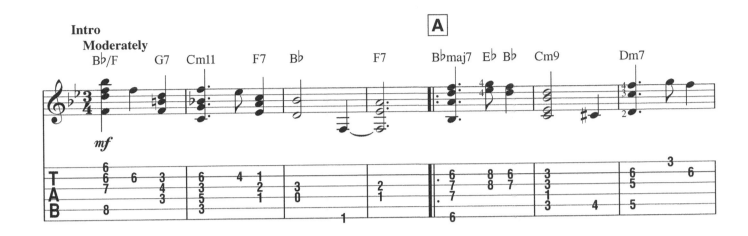

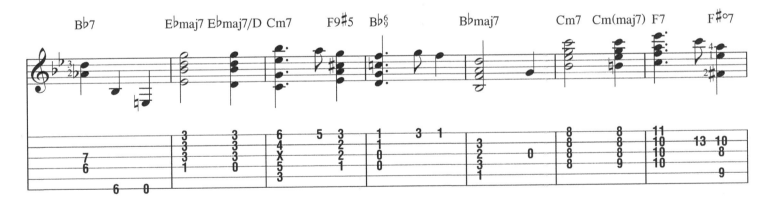

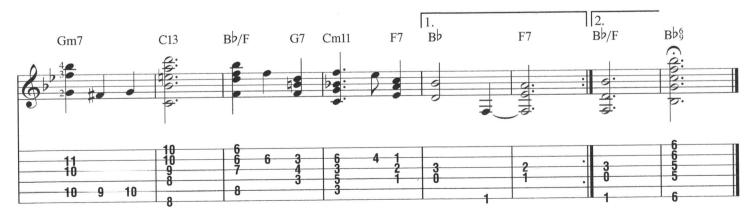

The Twelve Days of Christmas

Traditional English Carol

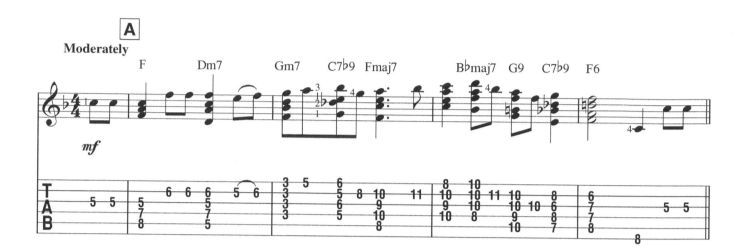

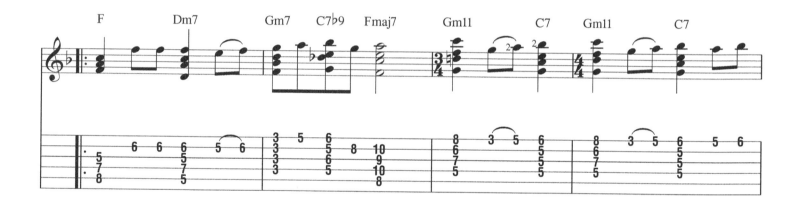

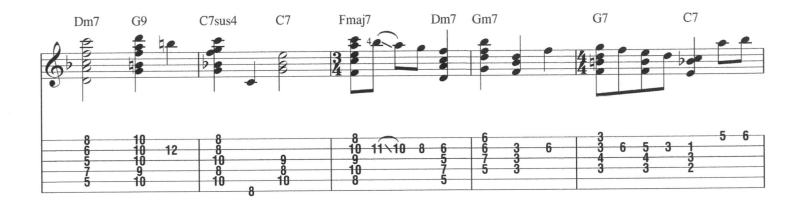

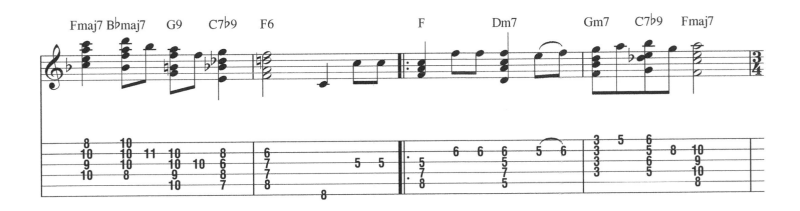

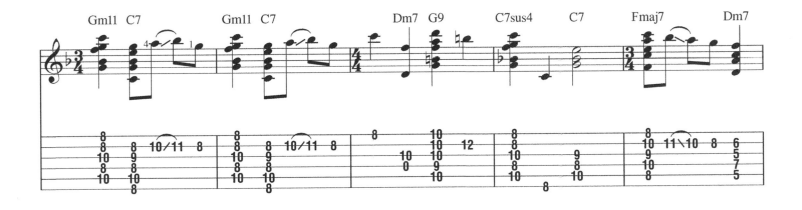

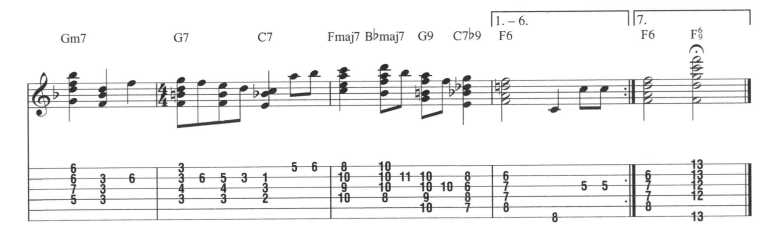

Toyland

Words by Glen MacDonough
Music by Victor Herbert

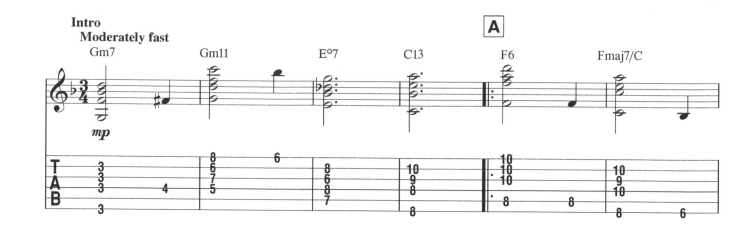

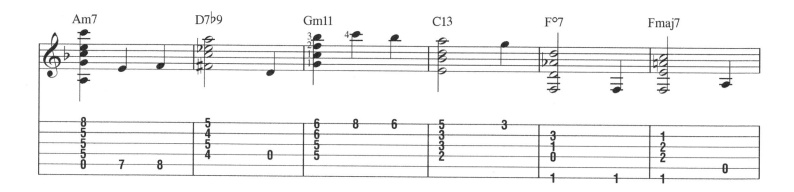

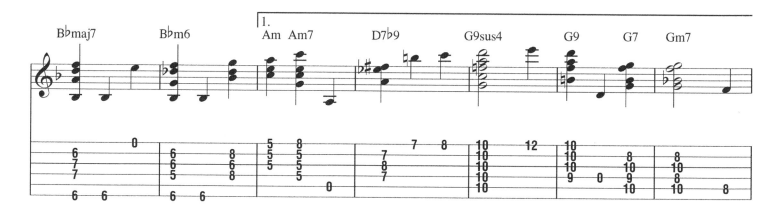

Up on the Housetop

Words and Music by B.R. Hanby

We Three Kings of Orient Are

Words and Music by John H. Hopkins, Jr.

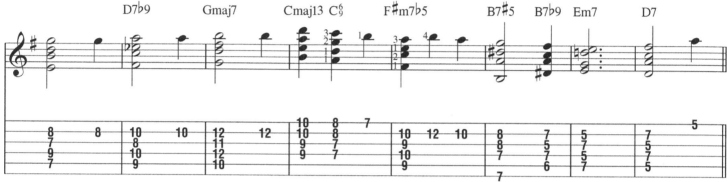

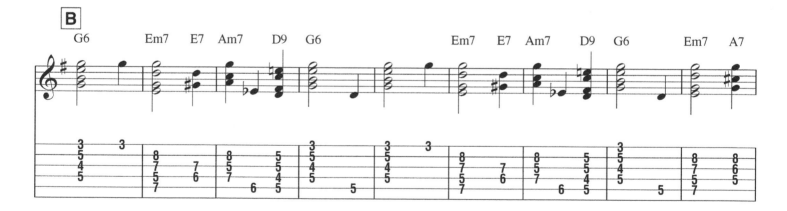

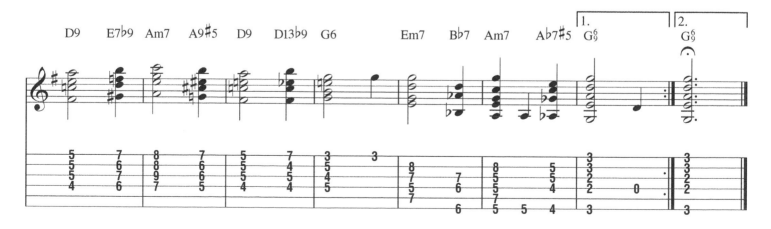

We Wish You a Merry Christmas

Traditional English Folksong

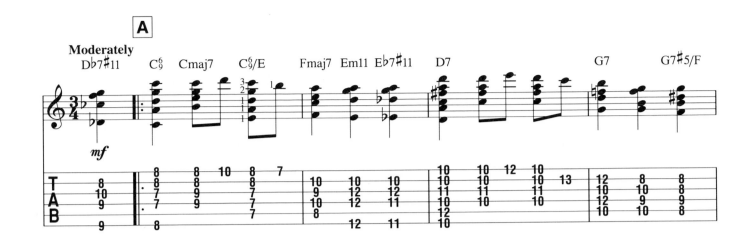

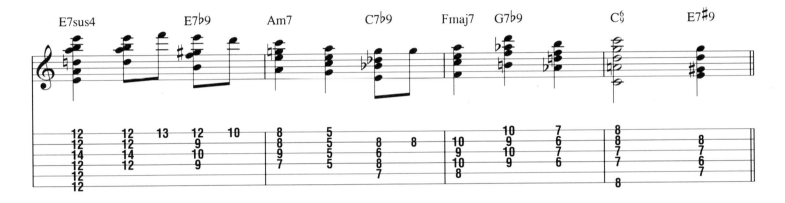

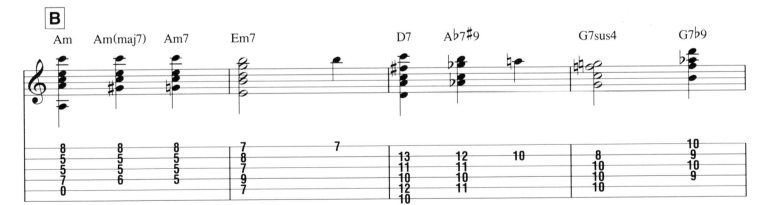

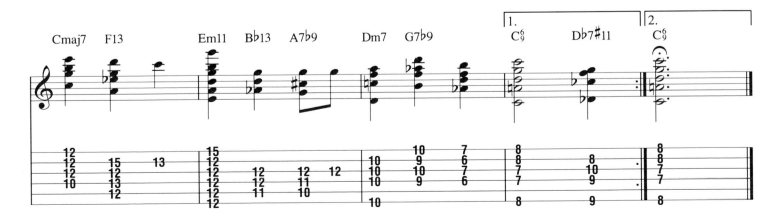

What Child Is This?

Words by William C. Dix
16th Century English Melody

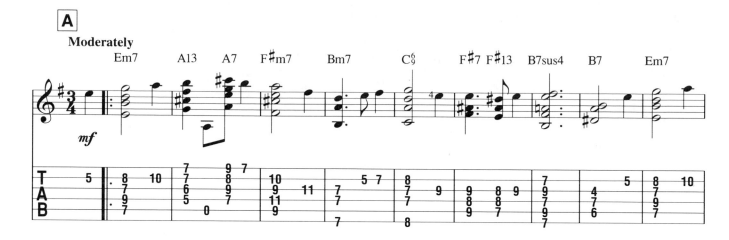

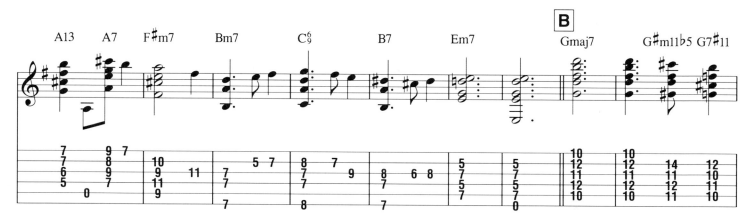

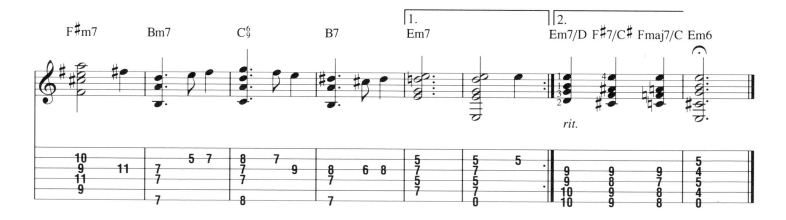

PLAY THE CLASSICS

JAZZ FOLIOS FOR GUITARISTS

BEST OF JAZZ GUITAR
by Wolf Marshall • Signature Licks
In this book/audio pack, Wolf Marshall provides a hands-on analysis of 10 of the most frequently played tunes in the jazz genre, as played by the leading guitarists of all time. Features: All the Things You Are • How Insensitive • I'll Remember April • So What • Yesterdays • and more.
00695586 Book/Online Audio................................ $29.99

GUITAR STANDARDS
Classic Jazz Masters Series
16 classic jazz guitar performances transcribed note for note with tablature: All of You (Kenny Burrell) • Easter Parade (Herb Ellis) • I'll Remember April (Grant Green) • Lover Man (Django Reinhardt) • Song for My Father (George Benson) • The Way You Look Tonight (Wes Montgomery) • and more. Includes a discography.
00699143 Guitar Transcriptions $14.95

JAZZ CLASSICS FOR SOLO GUITAR
arranged by Robert B. Yelin
This collection includes excellent chord melody arrangements in standard notation and tablature for 35 all-time jazz favorites: April in Paris • Cry Me a River • Day by Day • God Bless' the Child • It Might as Well Be Spring • Lover • My Romance • Nuages • Satin Doll • Tenderly • Unchained Melody • Wave • and more!
00699279 Solo Guitar $19.99

JAZZ FAVORITES FOR SOLO GUITAR
arranged by Robert B. Yelin
This fantastic 35-song collection includes lush chord melody arrangements in standard notation and tab: Autumn in New York • Call Me Irresponsible • How Deep Is the Ocean • I Could Write a Book • The Lady Is a Tramp • Mood Indigo • Polka Dots and Moonbeams • Solitude • Take the "A" Train • Where or When • more.
00699278 Solo Guitar $19.99

JAZZ GEMS FOR SOLO GUITAR
arranged by Robert B. Yelin
35 great solo arrangements of jazz classics, including: After You've Gone • Alice in Wonderland • The Christmas Song • Four • Meditation • Stompin' at the Savoy • Sweet and Lovely • Waltz for Debby • Yardbird Suite • You'll Never Walk Alone • You've Changed • and more.
00699617 Solo Guitar $19.99

JAZZ GUITAR BIBLE
The one book that has all of the jazz guitar classics transcribed note-for-note, with standard notation and tablature. Includes over 30 songs: Body and Soul • Girl Talk • I'll Remember April • In a Sentimental Mood • My Funny Valentine • Nuages • Satin Doll • So What • Stardust • Take Five • Tangerine • Yardbird Suite • and more.
00690466 Guitar Recorded Versions $24.99

JAZZ GUITAR CHORD MELODIES
arranged & performed by Dan Towey
This book/CD pack includes complete solo performances of 12 standards, including: All the Things You Are • Body and Soul • My Romance • How Insensitive • My One and Only Love • and more. The arrangements are performance level and range in difficulty from intermediate to advanced.
00698988 Book/CD Pack...................................... $19.95

JAZZ GUITAR PLAY-ALONG
Guitar Play-Along Volume 16
With this book/audio pack, all you have to do is follow the tab, listen to the online audio to hear how the guitar should sound, and then play along using the separate backing tracks. 8 songs: All Blues • Bluesette • Footprints • How Insensitive (Insensatez) • Misty • Satin Doll • Stella by Starlight • Tenor Madness.
00699584 Book/Online Audio............................... $16.99

JAZZ STANDARDS FOR FINGERSTYLE GUITAR
20 songs, including: All the Things You Are • Autumn Leaves • Bluesette • Body and Soul • Fly Me to the Moon • The Girl from Ipanema • How Insensitive • I've Grown Accustomed to Her Face • My Funny Valentine • Satin Doll • Stompin' at the Savoy • and more.
00699029 Fingerstyle Guitar $17.99

JAZZ STANDARDS FOR SOLO GUITAR
arranged by Robert B. Yelin
35 chord melody guitar arrangements, including: Ain't Misbehavin' • Autumn Leaves • Bewitched • Cherokee • Darn That Dream • Girl Talk • I've Got You Under My Skin • Lullaby of Birdland • My Funny Valentine • A Nightingale Sang in Berkeley Square • Stella by Starlight • The Very Thought of You • and more.
00699277 Solo Guitar $19.99

101 MUST-KNOW JAZZ LICKS
by Wolf Marshall
Add a jazz feel and flavor to your playing! 101 definitive licks, plus demonstration audio, from every major jazz guitar style, neatly organized into easy-to-use categories. They're all here: swing and pre-bop, bebop, post-bop modern jazz, hard bop and cool jazz, modal jazz, soul jazz and postmodern jazz.
00695433 Book/Online Audio............................... $19.99

HAL•LEONARD®

Visit Hal Leonard Online at **www.halleonard.com**

Prices, contents and availability subject to change without notice.

IMPROVE YOUR IMPROV
AND OTHER JAZZ TECHNIQUES WITH BOOKS FROM HAL LEONARD

JAZZ GUITAR
HAL LEONARD GUITAR METHOD
by Jeff Schroedl

The Hal Leonard Jazz Guitar Method is your complete guide to learning jazz guitar. This book uses real jazz songs to teach the basics of accompanying and improvising jazz guitar in the style of Wes Montgomery, Joe Pass, Tal Farlow, Charlie Christian, Pat Martino, Barney Kessel, Jim Hall, and many others.
00695359 Book/Online Audio $19.99

AMAZING PHRASING
50 WAYS TO IMPROVE YOUR
IMPROVISATIONAL SKILLS • *by Tom Kolb*

This book explores all the main components necessary for crafting well-balanced rhythmic and melodic phrases. It also explains how these phrases are put together to form cohesive solos. Many styles are covered – rock, blues, jazz, fusion, country, Latin, funk and more – and all of the concepts are backed up with musical examples.
00695583 Book/Online Audio $19.99

BEST OF JAZZ GUITAR
by Wolf Marshall • Signature Licks

In this book/CD pack, Wolf Marshall provides a hands-on analysis of 10 of the most frequently played tunes in the jazz genre, as played by the leading guitarists of all time. Each selection includes technical analysis and performance notes, biographical sketches, and authentic matching audio with backing tracks.
00695586 Book/CD Pack.. $24.95

CHORD-MELODY PHRASES FOR GUITAR

by Ron Eschete • REH ProLessons Series

Expand your chord-melody chops with these outstanding jazz phrases! This book covers: chord substitutions, chromatic movements, contrary motion, pedal tones, inner-voice movements, reharmonization techniques, and much more. Includes standard notation and tab, and a CD.
00695628 Book/CD Pack.. $17.99

CHORDS FOR JAZZ GUITAR
THE COMPLETE GUIDE TO COMPING,
CHORD MELODY AND CHORD SOLOING • *by Charlton Johnson*

This book/audio pack will teach you how to play jazz chords all over the fretboard in a variety of styles and progressions. It covers: voicings, progressions, jazz chord theory, comping, chord melody, chord soloing, voice leading and many more topics. The audio offers 98 full-band demo tracks. No tablature.
00695706 Book/Online Audio $19.95

FRETBOARD ROADMAPS – JAZZ GUITAR
THE ESSENTIAL GUITAR PATTERNS
THAT ALL THE PROS KNOW AND USE • *by Fred Sokolow*

This book will get guitarists playing lead & rhythm anywhere on the fretboard, in any key! It teaches a variety of lead guitar styles using moveable patterns, double-note licks, sliding pentatonics and more, through easy-to-follow diagrams and instructions. The online audio includes 54 full-demo tracks.
00695354 Book/Online Audio $15.99

JAZZ IMPROVISATION FOR GUITAR

by Les Wise • REH ProLessons Series

This book/audio will allow you to make the transition from playing disjointed scales and arpeggios to playing melodic jazz solos that maintain continuity and interest for the listener. Topics covered include: tension and resolution, major scale, melodic minor scale, and harmonic minor scale patterns, common licks and substitution techniques, creating altered tension, and more! Features standard notation and tab, and online audio.
00695657 Book/Online Audio $17.99

JAZZ RHYTHM GUITAR
THE COMPLETE GUIDE
by Jack Grassel

This book/CD pack will help rhythm guitarists better understand: chord symbols and voicings, comping styles and patterns, equipment, accessories and set-up, the fingerboard, chord theory, and much more. The accompanying CD includes 74 full-band tracks.
00695654 Book/CD Pack.. $19.95

JAZZ SOLOS FOR GUITAR

LEAD GUITAR IN THE STYLES OF TAL FARLOW,
BARNEY KESSEL, WES MONTGOMERY, JOE PASS, JOHNNY SMITH
by Les Wise

Examine the solo concepts of the masters with this book including phrase-by-phrase performance notes, tips on arpeggio substitution, scale substitution, tension and resolution, jazz-blues, chord soloing, and more. The audio includes full demonstration and rhythm-only tracks.
00695447 Book/Online Audio $19.99

100 JAZZ LESSONS
Guitar Lesson Goldmine Series
by John Heussenstamm and Paul Silbergleit

Featuring 100 individual modules covering a giant array of topics, each lesson includes detailed instruction with playing examples presented in standard notation and tablature. You'll also get extremely useful tips, scale diagrams, and more to reinforce your learning experience, plus audio featuring performance demos of all the examples in the book!
00696454 Book/Online Audio $24.99

101 MUST-KNOW JAZZ LICKS
A QUICK, EASY REFERENCE GUIDE
FOR ALL GUITARISTS • *by Wolf Marshall*

Here are 101 definitive licks, plus demonstration audio, from every major jazz guitar style, neatly organized into easy-to-use categories. They're all here: swing and pre-bop, bebop, post-bop modern jazz, hard bop and cool jazz, modal jazz, soul jazz and postmodern jazz. Includes an introduction, tips, and a list of suggested recordings.
00695433 Book/Online Audio $17.99

SWING AND BIG BAND GUITAR
FOUR-TO-THE-BAR COMPING IN THE STYLE OF
FREDDIE GREEN • *by Charlton Johnson*

This unique package teaches the essentials of swing and big band styles, including chord voicings, inversions, substitutions; time and groove, reading charts, chord reduction, and expansion; sample songs, patterns, progressions, and exercises; chord reference library; and online audio with over 50 full-demo examples. Uses chord grids – no tablature.
00695147 Book/Online Audio $19.99

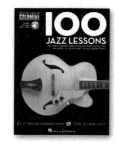

HAL•LEONARD®

Visit Hal Leonard Online at **www.halleonard.com**

*Prices, contents and availability
subject to change without notice.*